Are YOU Dateable?

Are YOU Dateable?

Toni Hodge

Copyright © 2010 by Toni Hodge

978-0-557-79103-3

All rights reserved. No part of this book may be reproduced, stored, or transmitted by any means—whether auditory, graphic, mechanical, or electronic—without written permission of both publisher and author, except in the case of brief excerpts used in critical articles and reviews. Unauthorized reproduction of any part of this work is illegal and is punishable by law.

*Dedicated to the loving memory of two of the most
dateable women I have ever known
Marion Louise Wilks (My Mother)
Sadie Lou Wilks (My Grandmother)*

Contents:

Acknowledgments	ix
Introduction	1
Chapter One Self-Preservation	5
Chapter Two Confidence	11
Chapter Three Control	15
Chapter Four Character	19
Chapter Five Get Yourself Together	25
Chapter Six Decide how you want to be treated And set a Goal	31
Chapter Seven Catering to the Male Ego	35
Chapter Eight Meeting the Man that Desire You	41

Chapter Nine Is your Man Dateable?	**45**
Chapter Ten A Successful Date for Two	**49**
The Finale	**53**

Acknowledgments

I thank God who I give all the credit for granting me the wisdom and courage to step out on faith to trust him in leading me to my destiny. Thank you to the wonderful women in my life that encouraged me to develop and realize the anointed gift from God that has been in my inner most beings from the beginning. Thank you for trusting me by sharing your personal stories, your pain, your most embarrassing moments and all your heartaches that led to both good and bad dating experiences. Thank you Shevita, Stephanie and Sheena for believing in me and listen to me go on and on and on about my dreams and my plans to reach my goals. Thank you to my behind the scene secret admirer (Chad), who secretly loves and supports me. Thank you to my friends and family members that have allowed me to analyze their relationships both good and bad, and trusted me to speak words of wisdom into their life.

Introduction

Ladies, it is my quest to redirect your thoughts, actions and motives toward dating. You think you can't find a man because you believe there are no good men available. Many have concluded that maybe it is not meant for them to meet a great guy and get married. The sole purpose of this book is to help the reader become aware of the fact that your lack of dates is because the woman that is looking back at you in your mirror is the biggest problem you have, not the men you are meeting. If you are having a problem meeting a man or dating, the only person you can fix or change is yourself.

Do you think you are dateable because you are attractive? Do you think you are dateable because you say you love yourself? Do you think you are dateable because you have a high powered career and you are highly paid? Do you think you are dateable because you have a college degree and maybe even a PhD? Do you think you are dateable because you haven't been married and don't have any children? Do you think you are dateable because you own your home and drive a luxury automobile? Do you think you are dateable because you attend church? Do you think you are dateable because you have good credit and money in the bank?

The answer to all your questions is NO! Absolutely Not! I know this will come as a shock to most women, but these are neither the qualities nor attributes that define you as being dateable. Now don't get it twisted, all of these qualities are great, but these are not the qualities that attract a man to a woman; unless you are walking around holding up a sign with your status displayed. When a man meets a woman for the very first time he does not know any of those things about her; so what makes him want to get to know you?

I started thinking about these questions and wondering why so many women with these qualifications say to me "I can't find a man", and some say, "There aren't any good men left". Many of you ask the question, if there are good men, then where are they? All of these questions have inundated women in our society all over the world. It is an age-old conversation in any woman's circle, whether you are rich or poor. Do I have all the answers? No not all of them, but what I do know for certain based on the revelation knowledge God has given me, and many years of research is this; most women are not examining themselves and they are approaching men, dating and relationships with the wrong motives, attitude and expectations.

Many of you with all of these qualifications look in your mirror every day, and you only see your status, you can only see your expensive designer clothes, your two hundred dollar sew in, your expensive Mac makeup, your manicured nails and toes, and your larger than life accomplishments and you think you got it going on. Women you are overlooking the fact that God created you to glorify him and then he gave you to man, so surly he has created a man in this universe that has been assigned to find you. Women, there are men looking for you, the question you should be asking is this: **Why can't he find Me?** What road blocks have you put up in your life that would prevent you from stepping into your destiny with the man God designed for you to love?

Women have we become so distracted by what we want for ourselves and perhaps forgotten our purpose and our divine assignment? Women your negative attitude towards men and dating, along with your long rap sheet of qualifications has overpowered your original assignment. Oh I hear you saying, I am not negative, well your words and your thoughts have power, so if you have declared, spoken or uttered these statements, "There aren't any good men", "It's hard to meet someone on my level", "All the good ones are married or in jail", "I don't have good luck with men", then you have built a barricade around you. Tell me how can you be successful in dating when you have spoken defeat before you can even get started? If a man happens by chance to find you, he would have to first tear down this wall of negativity and doubt that you have built up around you before he can date you.

Women we have become our own enemy, and it is a tragedy for those of us that really desire to love and be loved. Women how are you supposed to rise above what you have spoken into existence? How do you tear these barriers down to open the doors to being dateable? Do you realize that men and women alike enjoy being around places and environments where they feel welcome and comfortable? No one wants to be prejudged before they are given an opportunity to prove to you who they are.

I am convinced that there are dateable men waiting on you ladies to get it together, there are men everywhere you go and many are good dateable men. Ladies you can attract more flies with honey, so create an atmosphere for love to enter your personal space. Women are you ready to get your self-esteem on the high road; put your life in order, figure out what you want in a mate, what kind of man you desire and set some boundaries for dating?

This book will help to enlighten you on how you can date and meet the man who is looking for you with a positive outlook and attitude. Ladies stop looking for him and let him find you. This gift of wisdom God has given me, along with what I have learned from my own personal dating experiences, I gladly share with you all. I hope that what you read will bless all of you and I pray that in all that you read you get an understanding. Let's get started! This leads me to ask the question to all women that have a desire to meet a man and want to develop a healthy relationship that will lead to a future full of love and happiness, Are **YOU** Dateable?

Chapter One

Self-Preservation
Self –Esteem

You cannot be lonely if you like the person you're alone with. – **Dr. Wayne W. Dyer**

Being dateable is having high self-esteem and learning how to admire the person you see in your mirror. Self-esteem is to know and love who you are as well as believing that God has created a man that is looking for you. It is being assured that the man looking for you is not looking for just any woman, he is looking for you. It is the qualities, characteristics, gentleness and the inner spirit in you, that this man is seeking to find. Being dateable is also being ready and prepared when he finds you. It is about allowing yourself the time to discover who you are and becoming pleased with that woman in your mirror.

This chapter addresses the self-esteem issues many women are battling, their feelings of loneliness and being alone without a mate or a date. Before you can unequivocally declare you are dateable, you must first come face to face with the reality of why you are not approachable, kind, courteous, hopeful, and positive about dating. You need to address the concerns that you are having about being lonely. One of the reasons we as women have so many unproductive relationships is because we can't stand to be alone with ourselves. There are many women that can't stand their own company, but have the audacity to want a man to accompany them on that emotional roller coaster ride they are on.

Being dateable means examining yourself and cleaning your mind, body and soul of any negative energy before you began to invite anyone in your space. Did you know that thoughts travel and people can sense what you are thinking and feeling by your actions? Many women have a very negative attitude about relationships, dating, men and society as a whole. There are women that believe there are no good men available. Then you have women that believe if there were any good men left they would never meet them. There are women that believe all men are dogs. All this negative energy is like a magnet, it attracts men toward you that are negative, womanizers, disrespectful and it creates an atmosphere for unproductive relationships.

A dateable woman is not a negative women; she does not declare defeat before she starts her journey. Women if you have a negative attitude every time you meet a man, then you are your worst enemy. A dateable woman is not negative about her future; she has discovered what brings her to a place of contentment in her life and she is not mad at the world. This woman is pleased with the woman she has become before she invites anyone in her space. This woman has not become selfish and she is ready to share her life with the man God has created for her to love. This dateable woman is positive and she creates an environment that would draw this man toward her. This dateable woman knows that she can never rise above her thoughts, so her thoughts are positive and inviting.

Being dateable is being assured of your value, and it is learning how to admire the person you see in the mirror. It is learning how to enjoy your own company without it being a sad and lonely experience. Being dateable means coming face to face with the issues and challenges presented to you every day as a single woman without a mate or a date, and how you allow this to affect your self-esteem. This woman knows that if she can control her thoughts she will control her life, because whoever and whatever you think you are in your heart, that's who you are.

The way you think and feel about yourself will prove to be very important to being dateable, because your brain controls every cell in your body. I want you to search the depths of your heart and discover how much God loves you. When you discover your self-worth, you will find out that you are more powerful than most can ever imagine. Developing your self-esteem will be one of the most important challenges you will face as you start this journey to becoming dateable. One reason why developing your self-esteem is so important, is because you will be instructed to rearrange your thoughts in order to change the direction of your life as you take this journey with me. Your mirrors will not lie to you, what you see is what you get. Do you see a powerful, positive, attractive, successful woman of faith standing there looking back at you? Great, then walk in that truth everyday of your life, but if you are not feeling great about that woman in your mirror, then you are experiencing symptoms of low self-esteem.

Women ask yourselves questions such as, how do I feel about myself? Do I feel loved, inspiring, motivated, sexy, entrancing and indomitable? The way you think about yourself should inspire you to have confidence in what to expect from the universe. As your self-esteem begins to bud, please know that you are on your way to being dateable. Women did you know that, God created us to glorify, honor, and worship him. God has already created a mate to love and cherish you.

Women we never have to wonder if there are any good men available; just spend your time putting your mind, body and soul in order with your creator. Check to make sure your life pleases God before you are connected with your Adam. How can you be dateable if you don't know what you were created for? How can you be dateable if you don't love and respect yourself? How can you be dateable if you don't know your purpose in this life, and what you are anointed to do on this life journey?

Women let's start with getting to know yourself better. I want you to move past that image you see in the mirror and focus on the woman on the inside. First thing I suggest you do for your self- image, is to become your biggest fan, and the president of your very own fan club. Now, I know this is not going to be a problem with many of you self centered women; however if you can take your focus off of what you look like on the outside, and your good job, and concentrate on your messed up stank attitude we can break up some fallow ground.

Dating is opening up your heart to love, joy and pain. Your heart is at stake and you must guard your heart because within it lie's your soul. Proverbs 14:30, states "A sound heart is the life of the flesh". Have you ever noticed that when someone breaks your heart or hurt your feelings you feel bad all over? When your heart is hurting, you don't feel like eating, sleeping or working. This woman that you see in your mirror needs to be discovered by you, loved by you, and admired by you, before you begin to share her with someone else. When your heart is sound it means you will make sensible decisions for your life.

Ladies, I want you to know that you are deserving of love and happiness in every area of your life. Women should never accept from anyone disrespect which she does not deserve; and at all times you deserve the best. Take some time out of your busy schedule and write down a self-affirmation statement. This should be something you want to repeat to yourself on a daily basis. This affirmation can be something as simple as saying "I love me some me and nothing and no one will bring drama or disorder into my life, and I will not compromise my self-esteem for love". This affirmation alone should help boost your self-esteem. Place this in your mirror and repeat it daily.

Women we must feel superior and act superior, it doesn't matter what type of job you have or which career choice you have made. Your job is what you do, not who you are. Whatever you master in life make sure that you know more about yourself and what God your creator designed and assigned you to do on this side of the river; than you do about someone else. Shoot for the moon; it is ok if you land on the stars. Please always remember to never sacrifice your happiness to make someone else's day, if Mama ain't happy ain't nobody happy. Many times women know more about the man they are involved with, what he likes, their career and their girlfriends business than they know about themselves.

A dateable woman spends her time discovering her best qualities and finding out what makes her so special. At the end of the day and in the grand scheme of things, it is very important for you to know your self-worth. To be dateable, you must know without a shadow of a doubt that you are special and there is a man out there seeking to find a woman just like you. Ladies we were never designed to chase after the man we desire or at least the one we think is the man for us. You were created, designed and built for the man that is seeking to find you. The law of attraction states that, what is in you will seek you out. A dateable woman has already evaluated herself, and then she goes on to set standards and boundaries for her dating experiences. Everything you do in life has rules and regulations and you cannot date without having boundaries. Remember to treat yourself like royalty and others will respect how good you are to yourself.

Being dateable means knowing the proper manners to be successful in every setting. Ladies make an investment in your future and enroll in a class on etiquette. Proper etiquette classes will teach you some social manners. Social skills are important to being dateable. It is very difficult to know what the proper protocol is in various settings, if you have not been taught these things. A manners class will teach you social graces that will be an asset to you as you reorder your thinking and enhance your lifestyle. Women if you will allocate some time into putting your life in order, and focus on becoming the woman that God created you to blossom into, that man that you were created for will surly find you.

Self Esteem Checklist

1. Develop a personal relationship with God
2. Pray for Guidance
3. Build your Faith
4. Reorder your thinking
5. Value your Life
6. Appreciate your existence
7. Respect yourself
8. Love yourself
9. Cherish yourself
10. Define yourself by the word of God

Chapter Two

Confidence

You have to have confidence in your ability, and then be tough enough to follow through – **Rosalynn Carter**

Being dateable means being willing to challenge yourself to allow God to redirect your life. It is being confident in your ability to change your environment, friends, and attitude. If what you are doing is not working, and the places you are going are not productive; then it is time for a change. It has been said that "Only a fool continues to do the same thing over and over and expect different results". Confidence is that thing that assures you of your ability to succeed, and it is your support system.

This chapter on confidence speaks to your inner ability to succeed. When I think about confidence, which is nothing more than self-belief, I am reminded of the story of the turtle and the rabbit. In this story there is a race between a turtle and a rabbit, and the turtle is confident that he can win and so is the rabbit. The turtle does not look at the fact that he moves slower than the rabbit, or the fact that the rabbit has the ability to hop to the finish line. We know that in this story the rabbit is so confident that this race is going to be easy, that he stops along the way to eat and take a nap. While the rabbit is lingering around, the turtle continues steadfast on to win the race.

Self-confidence is being assured with your own ability; it is a state of trusting in yourself as the turtle did in this story. This simply means you can trust your judgment, regardless of the obstacles in your way. It means you can trust your decisions, and that you are confident in the choices you make for your life. I have always been told that if you don't stand for something you will fall for anything. When you are confident in your decisions, you are not easily swayed, regardless of the challenges you are facing. As you continue to build your self-esteem, have confidence in yourself, be firm about protecting your heart and the people you allow to enter your life.

As you become dateable, be confident that God loves you and he would not bring someone in your life that would hurt you or kill your dreams. As you become dateable, have confidence in your self-worth and recognize the fact that you can reach your goals. Women as you build confidence in yourself; you will become less afraid to allow God to reorder the direction of your life. Being dateable means being a risk taker, you will have to let go of your will and allow God to give you his will for your life. Confidence is trusting God to take control and you go along for the ride. Learning how to turn the wheel over to God is going to be a tough one, because we have this preconceived idea of what we think we want for our lives.

Being datable means allowing God to become your chauffeur and you the passenger; try really hard not to be a back seat driver. Having confidence in knowing that your life will change will give you the courage to set boundaries for the people which you allow in your space. Confidence is having the certainty to follow through to your divine destiny. Being dateable means trusting God while you prepare yourself for the man that God has designed to love and cherish you.

A dateable woman shows her self confidence by her behavior, body language, and how she speaks to others. One way to tell if your confidence is low is by governing your behavior based on what other people think. Women if you are afraid to get out and enjoy life, then it is because you stay in your comfort zone to avoid taking the risk of meeting someone that might persuade you to venture out. A dateable woman is confident because she always persists in the face of setbacks. She is not afraid to accept difficult challenges and she accepts responsibility for her actions.

A dateable woman knows that self confidence is extremely important in every aspect of her life. People that lack self confidence find it very problematic to become successful. Self confidence will keep you from being easily persuaded by someone who does not have your best interest in mind. Woman that are self confident inspire their peers, their children, and their men to excel in life.

Chapter Three

Control

He, who reigns within himself, and rules passions, desires, and fears, is more than a king is. – **John Milton**

Being dateable is being in control of your passions, desires and emotions. It is putting Godly standards in the forefront of your life to use as a guide to control your fears. These standards are the principles that God has already commanded us to live by. Control is exercising the power to direct our lives in the direction we want it to go. It is the power to exercise restraint and directing influences over our destiny. Control is learning how to create an atmosphere for great relationships.

Great relationships begin with us women being the masters of our passions and desires. We don't want to control the man; we want to control ourselves. We must control our own lives, our happiness, and our future. Women one of the reasons men can go from one woman to the next woman with ease, is because we have not learned how to control our emotions and passions. Women have you ever asked yourself and your girlfriends the question: Do I have stupid written across my forehead? If you have it proves that you recognize there is a problem with the amount of control you have over your life. The reason why you asked the question is because you are wondering why you continue to meet men that think you are stupid and underestimate your ability to control your destiny. There is something about the lack of control that you have over who you allow to enter into your space that is easily detected by men that seek woman that are vulnerable and weak.

Women we all know women that continuously allow themselves to date men that abuse them, use them, break them, and mold them into puppets on a string, all in the name of love. I know quite a few myself, and they all say to me, "he wasn't like that when we met, he changed". Well I hate to tell you, if he wasn't like that when you met and he changed into the man you despise and you are still with him, I see stupid on your forehead. Women if you don't control your destiny someone else will and drag you around by the nose your entire life. We must break the cycle of allowing men; love and lust control us, thus setting bad examples for our peers and our children. Women if you have ever wondered why women are attracted to the same kind of men that disrespect them over and over, the answer is because what is in you draws this breed of men to you, you are a prime target.

Being dateable means reigning within yourself. It means putting a system in place that will help you control your atmosphere and your raging hormones. One of the reasons we give our bodies to these undeserving men is because of our fears. Fear is simply a lack of faith in God. Women we need to give ourselves permission to say no to a man's desire to use our bodies like dumping grounds for his unwanted sperm. Oh I know you think I am tripping now, but think about it this way; in order to get what you want; you have to stop giving away yourself to every Tom, Dick and Harry because of your raging hormones. Being dateable means controlling your thoughts and emotions about love and sex.

Women when you have set boundaries for yourself and your precious body, (which is the temple of the Holy Ghost) you will always face opposition. As you become more approachable to men, please remember what is in you will seek you out, so you will meet men that refuse to respect your values. There are men out there that care nothing about the morals and standards you have put in place to control your unbalanced hormones. Being dateable is being equipped and eagerly ready to reject the undesirables that come your way. Women if you encounter a meeting with a disrespectful man, that cannot appreciate the principles and values you have put in place for yourself, tell him to get the hell out of your face. Don't waste your time trying to get him to see it your way.

A dateable woman is in control of her actions and does not accept an invitation from men that do not meet her standards. I have got to tell you ladies, I am so tired of women allowing certain holidays to control how they feel about themselves. It is time to stop throwing pity parties on Valentine's Day, Birthdays, Sweethearts Day, Christmas Eve and New Year's Eve. What is this foolishness about; if that isn't low self esteem then I don't know my name? So what! If you don't have a date on a holiday, is it really that serious? Why would you want to go out on a date with someone you don't want to be bothered with on any other day, just because it is your birthday? Women if I hear another song about birthday sex, I am going to get sick for real!!!!

Being dateable is being in control of your emotions. Here is a suggestion for your Holiday Blues. The next time your birthday and any other holiday that you get so emotional about comes around, take yourself out on the town. Women call and make reservations at your favorite restaurant; you know the one you only go to when someone else is paying, yeah that one. Get on the phone and order you a dozen of beautiful flowers, and when that night comes, get dressed in that outfit that you know you look real good in and hit the town. Ladies get out and enjoy your own company, and you just never know whom you might meet.

Being dateable means taking control of your own life, so when your man comes along you will already know how to enjoy yourself and have a great time. Women by this time you will have standards in place and if a man can't treat you the way that you treat yourself or better don't waste your time with him. Being dateable is learning how to set boundaries, and demand that any man you meet either meet you or beat you in how good you are to yourself. Take control over where your life is headed!

Chapter Four

Character

Be more concerned with your character than your reputation, because your character is what you really are, while your reputation is merely what others think you are. - **John R. Wooden**

Being dateable is being exceptional, charming, appealing, and eccentric while creating an atmosphere for love. Your character is the moral fiber that speaks to the world about the woman you really are. Since your image is the visual representation of one's self, the question to ask is what type of image am I projecting? As you build your self-esteem with the confidence that God controls your future and as you begin you're new dating experiences it will become very important for you to portray the proper image. How are you representing yourself? Take a very good look at yourself inside and out to determine where you are, and what you think about yourself now that you have enhanced your brand new self-esteem, and changed your outlook on dating to a more positive one.

Ladies did you know that men and women encounter a meeting every day, whether it is casual, business or personal? So you should ask yourself the question, when people are having an encounter with me, do they feel as though they have met someone that was exceptional? Have you ever encountered someone that walked into a room or passed you at a restaurant and you thought he or she was extraordinary? Their presence just took your breath away. This person's character was speaking loud and clear, and being in their presence was incomparable as well as pleasant. Their conversation was brilliant and when they left the room their reputation immediately became their image.

Ladies as you become dateable, it is important to develop an unmatched character that speaks volume. The law of attraction guarantees us, that what you send out is the same energy that will return to you. If you send out good vibrations loaded with charm, acceptance and confidence, the universe will yield itself to your heart's desire. Your personality is the magnet that draws men toward you. The man that God designed for you to meet will seek you out, if you give out the right vibrations. Develop an image that will precede your reputation and guarantee you an invitation to an extraordinary meeting. The statements you make with your mouth closed are the most profound ones, this is your eternal impression on the world. People will forget the words that you speak, but they will never forget your aura.

Being dateable means making all the right statements with a silent voice. Women we talk too much, we run our mouth out of season and in season. We need to allow God to teach us how to become virtuous women. A virtuous women is good, honorable and honest; she is worthy of the kind of man she desires. Women we must learn how to open our mouth, speaking only wisdom and kindness. Life experiences have a way of changing our desires, goals and dreams. If you have lived a life that was not so pretty in the past, that's okay, it does not have to determine your future.

Being dateable means rebuilding your reputation, it means changing your character. Changing courses is never easy, because we are always afraid of what people have to say about our past. We must learn how to view our selves the way God see us and not others. When God looks at us he sees our righteousness, he overlooks our faults and sees our needs. In the past if you were a stripper, prostitute, thief, drug addictive or a hypocrite, it does not matter to God, and if it doesn't matter to him, it should not matter to you. Women learn how to forgive yourself for your bad choices, God already has; let this be your past not you're present or future.

Being datable means to rebuild your character by changing the way you represent yourself. It is changing the way you normally do things. For example start with your conversations; if you use profanity with every other word, then you want to change your vocabulary. Being dateable is learning how to stop using the words bitch, hoe, and nigga when you greet your girlfriends, like these are terms of endearment. Women we have to stop the madness, we have to stop disrespecting one another before we can demand respect from others.

Being dateable is respecting ourselves when we leave our homes to go out to work or play. Women, would it be possible to please ask you to stop showing the crack of your ass to the world. Ladies, this is not good and it is not cute. A dateable woman knows what to wear and what not to wear. I have been there, we all sometimes go overkill with the sexy; however when we know better, then we should do better. Lets' do better! A dateable woman is a woman of integrity. She is respectful, honest and kind. Women, remember a few chapters back we talked about how we do things to ruin our character because of our lack of faith in God? Women, some of the things we lie about are totally unnecessary. We lie about money we say we don't have, money we say we need for an abortion, when we know we never were pregnant, money to get our car repaired, and money to get our hair, nails and feet done. Changing your character means to stop your lies and tricks.

Ladies, I realized that there are many times we have prayed and asked God for something, and it seems like his answer or deliverance is not coming quick enough. Well what happens is, we lower our standards and allow some jacked up brother with a few dollars cloud our vision. We get involved, he starts paying the bills and buying the groceries and we call it a blessing.

Women we have to learn how to hold on to God's promises until our change comes.

A dateable woman is a classy woman. She does not allow men to come in and use and abuse her for a few dollars. My mother use to say to me "daughter a man should not have a key to your house unless you have his last name". She would say to me, if I don't pay the rent I can't keep the key, so why should I give a man one for free.

A dateable woman is selective about who she let across her threshold. Women we need to be careful about letting any and every man you meet in your house. Some women let men in their homes, buy groceries, cook dinner for him and hand him the remote control, when you don't even know his last name and he don't know yours. Being dateable is being selective about who you bring around your children. Women some of these choices we are making don't make any sense. We let these users start sleeping over and disrespecting our homes, our children; and the next thing you know he's trying to lay with your son or daughter.

Being datable means building character that will stop you from lower your standards. It is all about changing your life and the direction you are headed. Women we need to stop making ourselves available for anything with a pair of pants to seek us out. I love it when men say to me "I can't afford you"; I am not offended, it lets me know that I am representing myself in such a way that he thinks my standards are too high for him to come up to. This man is telling me that he does not have high standards for himself and he would rather not have a challenge. Women the problem is this, he knows he can find a woman with low self-esteem and he can spend her money, drive her car, eat her food and sleep in her bed without any obligations required of him.

A dateable woman will allow God to reorder her thinking, set brand new standards while dating and respect herself and demand the men in her life do the same. Being dateable is being one of a kind. It is learning how to become elegant without being stuck-up, unfriendly and unkind. Women, if you want to build character you must respect yourself and others, be polite, learn to forgive, share and don't be selfish, and always practice good manners. Rebuild your character and reintroduce yourself to the world.

Chapter Five

Get Yourself Together

In the long run, we Shape our lives, and we Shape ourselves. The process never ends until we die, and the choices we make are ultimately our own responsibility.—**Eleanor Roosevelt**

A dateable woman possesses the knowledge how to shape her life continuously. It has been said "If you stay ready, you don't have to get ready". Getting yourself together is the single most important factor to being Dateable, because one of the most difficult challenges to accomplish is preparation. Some of you ladies are dealing with a lot of issues, and some have mental and emotional baggage that you have been carrying around since you broke up with your boyfriend in high school. I realize that some of the young ladies have not experienced marriage or children, and for you it is crucial that you start now getting yourself together. Getting yourself together is like cleaning out your junk drawer at home. It is about rearranging your life to assure that you are in the right lane and going in the right direction and staying steadfast on track.

Women it is important to redefine your dreams and goals after you have completed each assignment in life. It is imperative that we close the doors after bad relationships, unsuccessful marriages and any unproductive interruption we experience along the way. Women what we do is we hang on to these people and situations until someone else comes along. The proper way to make room for a dateable man to come into our lives is to empty our closet, clean out the drawers and dump out the trash before we can enter into another relationship free and clear of the memory of the last one.

I understand most women have experienced and overcome some of life's most difficult challenges, and yes we are survivors. One thing that happens to many women, is we have been so busy with the struggle of life, raising children, working, paying bills and just the simple task of keeping a roof over our families head and food on the table; we have not taken any time out for ourselves. I can tell you this because there was a time in my life; I was guilty of this myself. Once upon a time, I was guided to take a closer look at myself, who I was and even what I wanted to become. I did not realize any of my potentials until I was forced to decide what my next assignment in life was after my children were grown.

I thought my only calling in life was to be a good mother and grandmother, but then I said to myself, I can do that and more with my life, surly there is more to life than babysitting and raising more children. Women I came to realize that I was finished with that assignment, and I was successful doing the best I could with what I knew. Women we can have more than one dream, more than one career and more than one accomplishment in our life time.

Being dateable means getting yourself together before you younger ladies start having unplanned pregnancies, dropping out of high school or college and began to derail your future. Most of the time when we are dating we focus on what we want out of the man, and what he brings to the table. I want you to focus exclusively on what you bring to the table. Many people believe experience is the best teacher; I say it depends on the lesson you are trying to learn. In life it is good to obtain experience through other people's mistakes as well as your own. In many cases if I tell you the stove is hot, why not just believe me since you can clearly see I have a burned hand. Ladies many times in our life we are focused on others when it should be the woman in your mirror.

Getting yourself together sounds pretty simple doesn't it; after all you are just dealing with you and all your bad habits. We'll let's see, first in order to put your life on the right track you must know exactly what you want out of life, and which direction you want your life to take. You must become very familiar with the woman that you have blossomed into, as well as the woman you desire to be, and remember to keep your dreams before you daily. Getting yourself together depends solely on how you view yourself and how well you know yourself. Ladies make a list of things you like about yourself, and then make a list of all the things you would like to change or enhance about yourself, then allow God to shape your lives.

Being dateable means taking some time to get it together, before allowing love to find you. Don't expect someone to love you, if you are unhappy with that woman in your mirror. Stop thinking people should love you just the way you are, if you are a train wreck waiting to happen. How can you expect someone to like what you dislike about you? I know a lot of women say he will have to accept me the way that I am. Women, if you are unhappy with your life, the way you look, the way you dress and your inability to rise above your circumstances, why do you think someone else should be responsible for building your self-esteem and loving you? That is your responsibility exclusively.

Being dateable is mastering the art of dating yourself first. Start dating yourself; learn how to enjoy your company before you share your presence with someone else. Ladies stop talking about what you don't like, if you have never allowed yourself to experience anything. Being dateable means allowing yourself to be exposed to different cultures, lifestyles and different environments. Women once you get some exposure and some experiences, then you will be better informed on what you like and what you don't like. Ladies please allow yourself to live out your dreams and fantasies by traveling out of state and out of the country. There is nothing to fear, just take the first step and do it. Women you need to make your own discovery, you don't have to wait for a man to come along before you experience the finer things in life and many of the adventures this world has to offer. Stop expecting for someone else to come along and make all your dreams come true. You and you alone have the power to do so yourself. If you get out and start dating yourself, and enjoying life it is a guarantee you will meet a wonderful mate along the way.

    Women need to stop being so codependent on their girlfriends and you don't need a partner for everything you do. Try taking yourself to the movies and out to dinner at a five star restaurant. Treat yourself sometime, it's nice and you will be surprised how much you will enjoy your alone time with no one but you and your thoughts. Some of you can't do anything by yourself, grow up, my three-year-old granddaughter can go to the bathroom by herself and so can you. Learn how to walk alone and depend on yourself. If you are not good to yourself, it will be hard for you to clearly know when someone else mistreats you.

    Being dateable means being willing to make changes to your life. Change your hairstyle, buy sexy underwear and night gowns; you don't need a man in your life to shop at Victoria Secrets. Women look in the mirror and face the reality that some hairstyles, clothes and shoes have expired; please bury the dead. Learn how to cook, take gourmet-cooking classes, and buy a cookbook to sharpen your skills in the kitchen. Enroll in belly dancing classes for fun and exercise. Shop if you must, but be wise with your spending. Have fun, enjoy yourself and be safe. Enjoy your own company before you subject someone else to you. Learn how to date you first.

    A dateable woman can look in the mirror and be totally honest about her past, present and future. As you shape your life be honest with yourself. If you know you have a jacked up hair style or bad skin, make a note of it and start to work on this immediately. If you know you are twenty pounds overweight than you desire, do something about it. You can start a simple exercise program by walking every day, don't wait until your girlfriend starts, this is all about you, the woman in your mirror. Let's get a reality check; let's get started, and let's get ready and stay ready. Ladies keep your dreams and goals in front of you daily as a reminder of what you want and where you are going, the best way to get started is by getting some experience.

Chapter Six

Decide how you want to be treated And set a Goal

Control your destiny or somebody else will – ***Jack Waslh***

Being dateable means that you are making certain that you are being treated like a lady by any man you meet. Most women want a man to be kind and understanding, but at the same time she wants to know he is her protector. Maintaining your self-esteem is of a high importance, as you ponder over what you want out of life personally and professionally. Women you want to make sure you are dating someone that treats you a special way, like the queen you are. Being dateable means that you know for certain what you like and you have set boundaries that demand the ultimate respect. Dating is an emotional experience, because it is all about maters of the heart, but you must first start your dating experience using your brain before you tap into your emotions.

Women let us be real; we all like different characteristics in a man when we are in a relationship. Some of us like a man who is quiet and reserved and many like men that have a little thug in him. Many women like men that are direct and in control and many like a man that they can control. Some women like to be wined and dined, some like a quiet meal at home with their man, and many like a little bit of both. Women your preference in men is developed over a period of time in your life. We choose men based on what we have been exposed to as well as our previous experiences. Our environment, education and experiences set the stage for the relationships we enter into.

Ladies if you have treated yourself well then your standards for dating has already been established. And for those of you that are waiting on someone to come along to take you to the movies and out to eat, then you have neither standards nor a guide to determine how you enjoy being treated. Whatever your preference is will be determined by what you have become accustomed to. A dateable woman makes a list of what she likes and uses it as a guide. You can have whatever you want and whatever your heart desires. Ladies more importantly you should be thinking about life changing personalities and traits you want in the man you are going to date.

Women remember if you don't have any experience you can't truly say what you like. Set a standard for yourself, have some set ideas of how you want to be treated. When you meet someone and they do not measure up to what you desire in a mate, don't waste time by trying to change another individual to fit your expectations. You must accept that this is who they are and this is what they like and let it go, **learn how to move on quickly.** Step away from the man and let him go; don't try to change what another person see as right in his eyes; please let them be right and move on. Women as you get out and begin to enjoy your life, remember that every man, every date, and every encounter you have, and every path you cross is not going with you to destiny. We all have a destiny and we must make the right choice about which man we ride off into the sunset with. Please don't allow dream killers and negative people to ride your train to destiny.

Goals are set to give us something to work toward and setting goals encourage you to work harder. Ladies, now that you know who you are, what you like and dislike, and you are more than ever confident in yourself and your abilities; it is time to set some goals.

A dateable woman knows how important it is to be specific and she is willing to allow God to make the adjustments. Since the idea of setting a goal is to make sure you have a direction in which you would like your life to take, ladies please stop believing you are running out of time. As long as there is life there is hope. Time is not your enemy; it is on your side, it certainly is your friend. Setting goals can be fun, start with a short term goal and then long term goals, for example six months or two years and then move on to a five year plan. Make a list of goals you would like to accomplish in life, love and relationships. There isn't anything wrong with a New Year's resolution. Resolutions give you something to work toward, a starting point if you will. It's always a good idea to start the New Year with new ideas and new goals.

Chapter Seven

Catering to the Male Ego

The hardest thing to learn in life is which bridge to cross and which to burn.-
David Russell

Being dateable is acknowledging and understanding the male ego. Whether you want to believe it or not there is a male ego that exists in every man. All men have this self-image or opinion of themselves that promotes their self esteem. Women you must know that a man's ego is attached to his personality and his very unique behavior. Women it is important to learn everything there is to know about men, study them very closely. Know their weakness their strengths, likes as well as dislikes. Women study the nature of man so you will be able to understand them better. When we understand the dominant nature of a man it better prepares us for dating. This is not anything negative; the knowledge will empower you to have productive relationships.

Women I have five rules I use as a guide to approaching the male ego. A dateable woman is a very good judge of character, she doesn't talk too much, she allows her man to lead the conversation, she is not aggressive and she is not arguementive.

Rule #1 – Be a good judge of Character

A dateable woman is a good judge of character. Being a good judge of character means to be an authority on the character of an individual. Women it means learning your date and spending time doing a little research, find out first if he has a relationship with his God. Find out what kind of woman he is looking for, and if you fit his expectations. Many times we get caught up, and we are not listening to what men are telling us. Find out if he likes to work, travel or if he is a couch potato. Find out if he has bad or good credit, and if he spends his money wisely. When dating you need to become an expert so you will know what type of man you are dating. Many women get involved with men in relationships and find out later that the man is on drugs or an alcoholic after they have fallen in love and all caught up with their emotions.

Rule #2- Don't talk too much

A dateable woman doesn't talk too much. She understands that she has two ears and one mouth in order for her to listen and learn more and talk less. She knows how to keep her cool and not to respond to everything she see or hear. Women we must learn how to bridle our tongues, only a fool speaks everything that is on his mind. Women the more you talk prevents you fewer opportunities to hear what most men will reveal to you about themselves. If you are revealing everything about yourself, then there will be nothing for him to discover. Women the more he talks the more informed you are about him. One of the reasons we miss what men are telling us about them, is because we are not listening. If a man is not telling you with his mouth, he'll surly reveal to you loud and clear with his actions how he feels about you. Actions truly do speak louder than words.

Rule #3- Allow your date to lead the conversation

A dateable woman practices good manners and she is not afraid to be submissive to a man. She allows the man to lead the conversation, and she is patient enough to wait until it is her turn to voice her opinion. She approaches the male ego with caution, because she is not controlling and she is not rude. Women we want to know if we are going out with our future husband, so learn how to be modest with your conversations to get your questions answered. I believe you should know his intentions and goals for the future, but give the relationship time to take off first before going into a conversation about the future. Give the man time to tell you what is on his mind and what his intentions are.

Rule #4- Don't be Aggressive

A dateable woman is not the aggressor, because she is conscious of the dominate nature of a man. She knows that if she is aggressive he will see her as being hostile. She is assertive in a very gentle way. She is neither aggressive nor controlling. Women if you want to run a man off, just start running your mouth and being demanding, this will do it every time. Women we must learn how to allow the man to lead, stop trying to run everything.

Rule #5- Don't be Arguementive

A dateable woman is not arguementive, because she knows that a soft answer turns away wrath. She knows how to win friends and influence people by not bickering about every little thing. Women when you are dating or in a relationship, it is not necessary to argue and fight over the small stuff. If your date is misinformed about a subject or an event; it is not necessary to embarrass him by arguing about something that is so simple. It is ok if he is incorrect he will figure it out later.

Women, I want to teach you how to ask for what you want, without actually asking for it. Being dateable is mastering the male ego by talking less and listening more. In all relationships whether it is long term or short-term one, women must show their partner that you are a willing participant (it takes two to tangle). Now I know a lot of you ladies are not going to agree but that's ok, because you are probably the one's that say, "I can't find a good man", and you don't have one.

Being dateable is being mentally stable enough to sit down and hold an intelligent conversation without thinking you are all that and a bag of chips. It is learning how to be polite and not presenting yourself as a know it all. Men expect women to be the softer side of their lives. They are looking for a softer version of themselves. Someone that is resilient yet kind. Ladies let your conversations be soothing and calming; allow your man to speak and make decisions, while allowing him to make mistakes without you tearing him a new butt hole or making him feel smaller than a pea.

If your man is wrong about something, be supportive and say something like, it's ok baby, we will get it right the next time. Don't be aggressive and antagonizing by saying the usual I told you (Blah, Blah, Blah), just smile, listen, and shut the hell up. Please don't think I am saying be seen and not heard, just know when to hold them and when to fold them.

A positive and pleasant attitude creates an atmosphere for your man to feel safe with you. It makes him unafraid to share his secrets, fears and dreams. This attitude puts you in a position of power. There will be plenty of opportunities to voice your opinion and to be heard. Men are truly afraid of women; they don't want to be hurt, just like us. No one volunteers to enter a house where you know for sure there is an angry junk yard dog there ready to bark and tear you apart.

Women be nice and patient; meet his expectations of what a man thinks a woman should be. Remember you have the power;

he has stepped out of his comfort zone into your sweet, loving presence. He is ready to give you whatever you want because he trusts you. He is certain you have his best interest at heart. You will never have to ask him for anything he is going to give you whatever you need and want.

    A dateable woman makes her man feel that he is in a safe place with her. This man knows you are standing by his side when he needs you. He will give you the keys to his heart, house, and car and take care of all your needs. He has to, because he loves the way you make him feel. Ladies it is important for you to know that men stay with women because of how they make them feel. If you build him up and make him feel he is in a safe place and he can trust you, you can have whatever you want and never have to ask him for anything. Your man will be singing Bill Withers song "If it feels this good being used, then use me up".

Chapter Eight

Meeting the Man that Desire You

Even if you are on the right track you will get run over if you sit there. – **Will Rogers**

Being datable is the art of knowing how to date. Growing up in Memphis, I was taught how to ride the bus as a young girl. I learned if I was going downtown; I needed to get a schedule of that bus route and times. I also learned when traveling downtown, uptown or out of town, it was my responsibility to get on the right bus, right train, and the right plane, get in the right lane and on the right highway heading in the right direction. Well, I am certainly not saying men are like busses, I am simply saying know the direction in which you want to go and decide how you want to get there and with whom.

Taking responsibility for your life, love and happiness is essential to being dateable. I have noticed a lot of woman want to blame the man when something goes wrong. The only person responsible for your happiness is you. You cannot afford to put that responsibility into anyone else's hand. Your number one job is to take control of whom and what you allow to come into your life. Let's begin with who you desire, where to meet him and how to meet him. I know in the beginning of this journey you may take a wrong turn, but it's ok as long as you can find your way back home. If you make a bad choice, quickly let the man go and move on. Don't stay on the bus if you know it is headed in the wrong direction.

Who-Decide who you want to meet, meaning if you want a man that's tall, dark and handsome, or slim, fat or thick? Decide whether you desire a man that is a doctor, lawyer, engineer, blue collar worker or maybe an entrepreneur with a lot of money. Maybe your desire is a man that smokes and drinks or one that does not. Who do you desire to date? Is this man dateable? The choice is truly yours, your desire should be to meet someone that you can communicate and relate to you on many levels. Maybe someone with the same goals or someone you can relate to professionally. Your desire should be for a man that has the same interest and passions you have. Don't desire a couch potato if you like to travel, because you will find yourself continuing to take trips alone or with your girlfriend as before.

Where- Ladies I want you to say to yourself, well where do I meet this man? Where is he? Where does he hang out? Is he at the mall, grocery store, or laundry mat? Women, there are men everywhere you go, It is important for you to be creative. First step is to get out of the house; I need you to stop having favorite TV shows that you cannot miss. Invest in a DVR from your cable provider or buy a DVD player/recorder and record your favorite shows, you can get back to them later. You must be willing to become venturous; you must become a social butterfly. I need you to make yourself available for this man to find you. We are not in search of them, they are looking for us, and I want you to get out and enjoy your life.

Men are everywhere you go, except for the woman's bathroom, hopefully. Men hangout at places likes golf ranges, sports bars, house parties, work, etc. I am recommending you stay away from the club. Ladies, would you be willing to learn new hobbies? Take up a new sport, learn how to play golf, tennis or something you have always wanted to learn and did not. Join local social clubs; go to jazz and music festivals, tennis matches, basketball games and football games. Get involved in your community; join the public, political and civic organizations. Get involved; volunteer to work on political campaigns. Get out and start enjoying your life, you are not looking for a man, he is looking for you.

I hear women say all the time they can't meet any good men. Well, if that's what you believe, then so be it. You can never rise above your thoughts. Honestly I have never had that problem and never will, because I don't think that way. The key is to start living and enjoying your life. Become a source of information about what's going on in your community. Search the Internet; check the newspapers, sign up for updates of community events to be emailed to you. Find out what's coming to your town that you would like to checkout. Go to a show, concerts, and plays, you don't need a date and don't' always take a girlfriend every time you go out. Why take the competion with you every time you leave the house. Ladies, you have already determined what it is that you like, so go for it. Get out there and enjoy what your city, your state and your country have to offer. The world is your playground, get out there mix, mingle and enjoy.

A dateable woman knows how to put her best foot forward, by being amazing, subtle yet enchanting. As you enter any room, make sure you are approachable. Smile, speak, flirt but don't be obvious or seem overly aggressive. Be very polite and charming during your conversations. Accentuate your best qualities, without showing your bare necessities and be careful not to have any wardrobe malfunctions. Simply put, wear a good bra, you don't want those girls sagging or jumping out. If you have nice legs, it's ok to show them without your dress stopping at your butt. I think every woman should own a nice pair of pumps. Ladies pull out your sex appeal without being smutty; learn how to dress for success. Men love to be in the presence of a beautifully dressed woman with a great personality; trust me you are making him look good. You never know when Mr. Right is watching or listening.

Chapter Nine

Is your Man Dateable?

Men are like wine, some turn to vinegar, but the best improve with age. –
Pope John XXIII

Being dateable means being wise enough to know whether the man you meet is datable. Women how can you tell if the man you are dating is datable? Men can be very complicated at times. Man was created with a very unique nature. What happens is many men we encounter in this society come from all walks of life, some two parent homes, single parent homes and even homes where there are same sex parents. Men have the nature that God gave them and then they have the morals and standards that their mother did or did not give them. Throughout history man has been known to be the protector, provider and the leader; he is the head and not the tail. It is the anatomy of a man to be different in nature, so it is imperative to find out if he has matured and what qualifications, traits, strengths and wisdom he has acquired in order to be successful in being dateable.

A dateable man that was reared in a home with a mother and a father should have been taught what a man's role is in a relationship. Does he know how to respect the woman he is dating? He should know that he is the head of his household; and this man should know that it is his responsibility to love his wife like Christ loved the church, and that he gave his life for it. This dateable man knows that you don't wait until you get married before you start treating this queen like a queen. His mother should have taught him that women are emotional beings and he must tap into his sensitivity to deal with a woman. This dateable man should have the knowledge that he also must help out at home with cleaning, cooking and washing. This man's father should have taught him that getting a woman pregnant does not make him a man; it only makes him a sperm donor.

A man that was reared by a single woman should have the capabilities to cater to the female ego. He knows what makes her cry and what makes her laugh. This man is a strong man, because he's had to be the man at home growing up with his mother. This man should know that he needs to cut the grass and take out the garbage. He knows how important it is for his mother to get a card and a gift on Mother's Day and special occasions. This dateable man knows how to cook, clean and wash clothes.

A dateable man is a teachable man. This man doesn't mind allowing someone teach him the steps to becoming successful. This man is eager to learn how to become a better man. He does not lay in every hole he comes across just to get his kicks off. He is selective about the women he dates. A dateable man reads and spends time discovering what his purpose in life is. He wants to please God and his woman by obtaining the knowledge how to through God's word. He studies and works hard at becoming successful in every aspect of his life.

A dateable man is a man that is mentally stable. A mentally stable man makes wise decisions for himself and his family. Adam, who was the first man was wise; he also was intelligent and unique; In the Garden of Eden, Adam named all the animals. A dateable man makes intelligent decisions for his life and the people involved with him. This man is not a foolish man. This man is not a mama's boy. He is not waiting on his mama to tell him who to date. A dateable man makes wise choices with his money, and his credit is good. He is intelligent enough to lead and he is wise enough to know when to follow.

A dateable man knows he must pray. This man is dateable because he understands how important it is to have a prayer life with his God. He prays for guidance and he know that a good man's steps are ordered by God. This man is dateable because he prays for his family, his children, his relationships and himself. A dateable man honors his mother and his father. His relationship with his God has prepared him to be respectful and honorable in all his actions.

A dateable man knows how to love the woman that God made for him. He honors her presence in his life. He believes that when a man finds a wife he finds favor with God. A dateable man is looking for a wife not a one night stand, not someone to shack up with, and not some low self esteem woman that he can use and abuse. A dateable man wants a dateable woman. A dateable man is a man that realizes he is a masterpiece made by God. God gave the order to man in the beginning to be responsible; so if you meet a man and he is not responsible, not teachable, not wise, and not prayerful then he is not a dateable man.

Chapter Ten

A Successful Date for Two

I have not failed; I've just found 10,000 ways that won't work. –**Thomas Alva Edison**

Being dateable knows that dating is a win or lose experience. Dating means taking risk, and sometimes you win and sometimes you lose. A dateable woman is a prayerful woman. She prays for guidance and direction on how to keep her relationships sacred before God. This chapter will address courtesies in a relationship and how to win more than you lose. Ladies remember that you attract into your life what you think about, so change your thoughts and change your life.

When going out on a date the first thing you want to remember is that you are the guest so always be polite and enchanting. Women we must understand and learn to embrace the fact that men are visual, that's just the way they are; however at the same time we are also, only not as extreme as them. Women, we all have to pass the look test first, and if you are what he is looking for, and he is what you are looking for, then the two of you can continue from this point on. Women so the first thing you do is to appeal to the male sensitivity, make sure you are easy on the eyes, very nice to look at when going out on a date. I know many of you may not like this, but embrace this reality.

Once a man has a visual, he can take it from there to find out your intellect. I am not suggesting that you dress sleazy or that you dress seductive; just be classy and appealing. Women dress in a way that he want come to the conclusion that you are a nun or a ghetto queen. A dateable woman should be charming and amazing. Make him want you in every way. I didn't say give yourself to him, I said make him want you, desire you and need you. Make him feel like he just hit the lottery, like he's got the winning Powerball ticket. Make him feel like he needs you in his life and he can't live without you.

A dateable woman is a great host in any environment. Once you have your date's attention you are in charge and everything that happens after this is in your control. Now he is at your mercy, and he wants you to be gentle. This man is treating you to a night out and you are only gracing him with your wonderful presence and charm. He likes being around you because of the way you make him feel about himself. It is no charge, stop thinking you have to pay up at the end of the night. All he wants from you is for you to be polite and give him the attention he needs. Women I am not in an allusion, I realize that there are men that are looking for one thing, and that's why you need to be a good judge of character; and if by chance one slip through the cracks and you find yourself out on a date with this heathen just say no to sex at the end of night.

A dateable woman makes good choices when dating and she knows when to hold them and when to fold them. After you have been on many dates with him, movies, walks in the park, etc., don't be afraid to give a little because you stand to gain a lot. What I mean by giving a little is for you to entertain at home after you have gotten to know him and trust him in your home. The first home entertainment date should be on you, don't go to his house; stay in your comfort zone. Cook for your date; let him know what kind of a woman you are. Show him you are willing to cater to him. Prepare his plate; make him feel like a king. You treat this time, buy groceries and fix him a nice home cooked meal.

Women cooking for your man lets him know you are not a gold digger and you give as well as receive. Impress him by showing off your culinary skills and offer to give him the leftovers to take to work for his lunch the next day. Show him in every way that you are giving and not selfish. Be sweet and understanding and show him your generous nature. Women no worries, you will not end up with the short end of the stick. Keep reading, I will teach you how to get your rewards. Ladies always show your willingness to give; you will always come out on top. Women remember to keep your standards high and don't cook for men that can't afford to buy you a home, and groceries in the future, don't waste your time and a good meal on a lazy bum. Make sure you are making the right investment.

Being dateable is being wise enough to know that men make it a habit to return to their comfort zones. Have you ever noticed that most men unlike many women have been going to the same barber since they were little boys? Contrary to popular belief men are loyal to situations and people they trust. Here is a secret for you; Men are very emotional and sensitive. One sure way to keep your man is to always create an atmosphere of comfort and trust; No Drama! Drama at home will make him seek a place of comfort some place other than home. He may come back home to you, but your man will surly step out and find someone that can make him feel comfortable.

The Finale

I hope our wisdom will grow with our power, and teach us, that the less we use our power the greater it will be. –
Thomas Jefferson

A relationship between two people can be productive or counterproductive. Productive and counterproductive behavior has a major impact on successful dating. These two behavior patterns can make or break a relationship between a man and a woman. One major reason is because, we all want to know if we are dateable, we want to know if I am right for him and if he is right for me. Based on some simple truths that we all grew up on, we look for people that have what we call "home training". I believe we all can agree we have met plenty of adults with no home training, no manners, and no insight on what or how a man or woman should behave in a relationship.

The behavior patterns of an adult should be consistent with ones age and education, which would lead to healthy and productive relationships. With a growing number of dating sites, and match making services related to screening a suitable date, the dating environments have swamped the nation with an unprecedented amount of unproductive hookups and a lot of unnecessary extra sexual encounters with the wrong people. In relation to dating, productive and unproductive behaviors can no longer go unnoticed.

Productive behavior is the manner in which one behaves in a positive, motivated fashion. This behavior pertains to a person's actions as they constitute a means of evaluation as it relates to any relationship. I believe that proper communication and direction is two of the most dominant forces between success and failure within your dating experiences. Since people are all different, they cannot be communicated with alike. Being dateable is being in control of your thoughts, conversation, and emotions. Mature adults that are dateable will exemplify character, poise, respect and dignity that spell good home training.

Productive behavior can be achieved in a relationship by creating an environment for increased happiness while dating. A man or a woman can be successful when dating if sound relationships are built from the beginning. Getting a relationship off to a solid productive start is the key to success when dating. The beginning of a relationship is where we put everything on the table, the good, the bad, and the ugly. There is no need for secrets, lies or deception. This is the place where everyone has a clean slate and what you do after this will determine the direction the relationship will head. It is your choice whether you will be in a productive or counterproductive relationship. Women if you guard your heart and continue to be selective about your choices for dating, you will have continued success in dating. Women we all want to be loved, but by the right man, we don't want to waste time on the wrong one, so make your choices prayerfully and carefully.

Counterproductive behavior can be derived from something as simple as a bad attitude. Women and men alike are having encounters with each other with negative energy. Women if you don't want to be bothered do the world a favor and stay at home with your bad attitude. Many times women we are out meeting people and we have a bad attitude and we meet men that are negative toward women that are successful and intelligent. I told you what was in you would seek you out; all this negative energy is counterproductive.

Many women are mad at the world, because they did not take care of business early in life. These women are angry because they did not guard their hearts and they allowed some disrespecting man to slither into their life and rip them of their dignity. Many women have given birth to babies that men don't want and refuse to provide for them, and it is everybody's fault that they are having a bad day and an unproductive life. When we are negative and have become weary in our well doing, we are driving up the rates of chronic disease and creating an unproductive atmosphere for dating. Women we are working hard and raising children but we need to find a way to stay positive and productive in order to be successful. Hard work and strong work ethic is a good thing, but it can inadvertently have long-term negative consequences on the wrong behavior.

Being dateable is a mind over matter experience. It is that positive attitude and positive outlook that will produce successful relationships. Women after reading this book, I want you to begin to speak into your future with words of positivity and you will invite good men, love and happiness into your space. The most important job you have in your life is to take responsibility for your happiness. Ladies please stop giving this responsibility to the men in your life. Women let nothing exalt itself over the will of God for your life; which is to prosper and be in good health even as your souls prosper.

Women if you want to be dateable and you want a man in your life to date, it is imperative for you to replace everything in your life that is negative with positive energy. Your thoughts about dating, love, life and happiness must change. Women you must enlarge your expectations in order to receive the things in life that you desire for your future. Women start preparing yourself for the love that you desire. When a woman is pregnant with child, she has nine months or less to prepare herself and her environment for what she is expecting. Women if you believe that God has created a man for you, start preparing yourself for him to find you.

Ladies, your negative attitude toward men and dating is like a cross to a vampire. Women no man is coming into your negative space if you don't change your thoughts, and if you are lucky enough to get a date it won't last for long. Start with waking up in the morning with the attitude that you are ready for something great to happen. You will get what you are looking for, because for every action there is a reaction. Women you can speak into existence what you want, the power of the spoken word is your key to being dateable. Ladies if you can believe, visualize and create an environment for your man to seek you out, you will find it very easy to meet good dateable men. – The End

Made in the USA
Monee, IL
03 May 2026